COUNT

Butch Thomas

COUNT

Thomas Publishing Company
c/o Cardjazz, INC

Atlanta, Georgia 30308

ISBN-978-0-963030252

Cardjazz1@yahoo.com

Novice Edition

My book is dedicated to the Atlanta-Fulton Public Library System. The importance of computers in libraries played a vital role in the completion of this book. It allowed me to set up a routine mind set, and provided access to programs and databases at a faster communication speed. 90% of the book was authored at the library.

POINT COUNTING

WHERE THE ACTION IS

♠ ♥ Contents ♦ ♣

Counting

Counting is deeply rooted in every space of bridge. It occupies more than ½ of each player's concentration. As it relates to evaluating your High Card Points (HCP), it is more of a habit than a skill. Players who practice repeatedly to count points with speed and accuracy should be able to improve their bridge memory. In turn, better memory will produce better bridge.

There are various counting bridge measurements.

Players should count their cards after the deal to make sure the hand is ready to go with 13 cards.

Players should count points during the auction.

Players should count trump and discards during the action of play.
Players should count HCP's in Dummy, and add the total to their hand count.

Declarer and Defender should count possible winners and losers. And, players should calculate how many tricks required to make or to lose their contract.

Players should count tricks collected after the game.

Players should compare their score with the opponent to verify trick count.

Players should review the score to calculate how many points are needed to win game.

The purpose of this book will focus on counting points before, during and after the auction. Let's play this out. Review the following table:

High Card Points (HCP's)
Ace = 4   King = 3
Queen = 2   Jack = 1

This counting chart is sometimes called the Royal Family, i.e. A+K+Q+J=10

Here is a formula to help you with your
Point Count treasure hunt.

Player's Personal Point Count

Auction (Bidding) Point Count

Dummy's Point Count

This Bridge Odyssey offers 3 main paths for
counting points. As a **Player's Hand** is looked
over for HCP's, cards are sorted from strength to
weakness. The **Auction** allows players to calculate
points around the card table from each bid. And, the
Dummy's Hand goes down on the table for every
player to examine, allowing players to combine
points from 2 hands. For the purpose of this book,
is to link together count activities to guide novice
bridge players through each phase. In order to get a
sense of point counting around the table, a certain
amount of instinct is required. It will all come
together if a player can locate who, when, where,
why and how to find the HCPs hiding places as
well as the distributional points. During the first
round of bidding, you should know who is the
player leading the bidding, and based on your hand,
why? You also should know where to look for
help. In addition, you should know when to shut
up. How to use this information comes later. With

a little quick surgery, your offensive game will say, HELLO, and your defensive game will say, Let's Go. If a bridge player knows where the points are, bidding and card playing can improve with the quickness.

Player's Hand

Auction

Dummy

Counting puts your
Bridge Game in Turn-Around

Personal Point Count - The first point is counted from a hand of 13. A player needs to use the classic method on page 7 & 11. Although modern day bridge has shifted toward using various conventions, counting is the central bridge activity.

Review the following hands

A) ♠ T 9 8 7 6   (B ♠ J T 9 6 4 2   (C)♠ Q J 8 6 5
   ♥ 4   ♥ 8 5 3   ♥ K 7 3
   ♦ T 9 3   ♦ A 6   ♦ T 8
   ♣ 7 4 3 2   ♣ 8 2   ♣ Q 8 4

(D) ♠ A K J 8 6   (E) ♠ A K Q J 7 5   (F) ♠ A K J 8 6
   ♥ A   ♥ A K 7   ♥ A K 7
   ♦ A K 8   ♦ A 6   ♦ A K
   ♣ K Q T 5   ♣ 8 2   ♣ Q 8 4

(A)   This hand is a Yarborough. It does not contain any points. Pass

(B)   This hand has 5 points with a useless Doubleton. Pass

(C)   This hand contains 8 HCP's. Pass

(D) This hand is worth 26 points. There are 24 in high cards, and 2 points for the singleton. Open

(E) This hand contains 23 points (21 in high cards points and 2 for each Doubleton). Open

(F) This hand is worth only 24 points. Open

Distributional Points
(Singleton= 1, Doubleton=2, Void=3)

This aspect of counting applies to Suit bidding. It is based on length, shortness and/or the very existence of a suit. For example, if holding a singleton Jack of Trump for partner, it may have the usual one point value. Without protection, it could be a winner or loser. Or, if holding a Jack of another suit **(not trump)** for partner, it could have two points spilling over to create ruff winners. And, as a singleton Jack for the opponent, it could be scooped up as a discard. Consequently, it could be a loser with zero point value.

Another way for distributional points to **usurp** HCP's is if Declarer has a Void, and the opponents have the Royal Family (AKQJ) as the Void Suit. The 10 points is transferred to Declarer's hand, and the AKQJ is ruffed up by TRUMP. So, it comes down to ruffing potential verses discard potential. Leave some wiggle room when counting these intangible points. They are slippery when competing for high level bids.

Player A - Spade Suit: AKJT642 **Long Suit**
Only 6 Spades are left among the other 3 players.

Player B - Spades Suit: Q9   **Short Suit**
Since the Queen is not protected, the 2 points is shifted to the player with the long suit.

Review point count in these examples?

♠	♥	♦	♣ TOTAL
A92	T753	K74	742 = 7
JT63	64	A83	KT86 = 9
Q85	98	QJT96	A83 = 10
K74	AKQJ2	52	AQJ = 19
94	A85	T74	AK642 = 12
QJT8	J743	J963	5 = 6
AK7	KQ2	A852	873 = 16
6532	T92	KQ	QJT9 = 6
T2	J63	KJT74	A76 = 9
J9	95	A983	QJT82 = 9
Q8654	KQT7	65	54 = 9
AK74	A842	Q2	K93 = 15

Point Count Chart

	Open	Response	Overcall
1 Club ----	13 - 14		
Diamond -------			7 - 10
Heart --------		6 - 9	7 - 10
Spade ---------		6 - 9	
1 No Trump -	15 - 17	8 - 10	10 - 17
Double -----------		13 - 19	
2 Clubs -----	-22 –24		6 - 13
2 No Trump -	21-- 23		
2 Diamonds ---	6 - 9		7 - 17
Hearts			
Spades			
3 Clubs -----	6 - 9		
Diamonds			0 - 10
Hearts			
Spades			
3 No Trump -	24 – 25		
4 Clubs			13 - 14

(left margin, vertical:) First Round Opening Bids

Besides Pass, a player will bid one of the above

Auction (Bidding) Point Count

The first round of bidding will detail point count information. Since there are only 40 points per deal to consider, a good chunk can be found during this part of the auction. Importantly, it does not matter how much bridge experience a player has, the first round is the point count round. Counting levels the playing field so that novice players will have a fighting chance to compete.

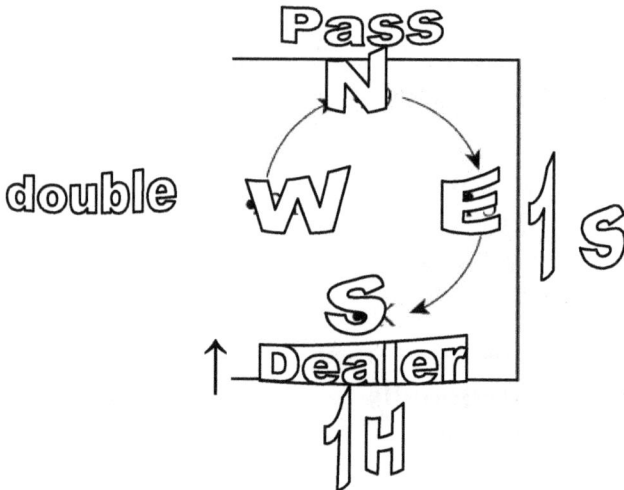

South West East
1H + Double + 1S
13+13+6=32 Points

After counting the least amount of points for East, most of the 40pts are found during round one.

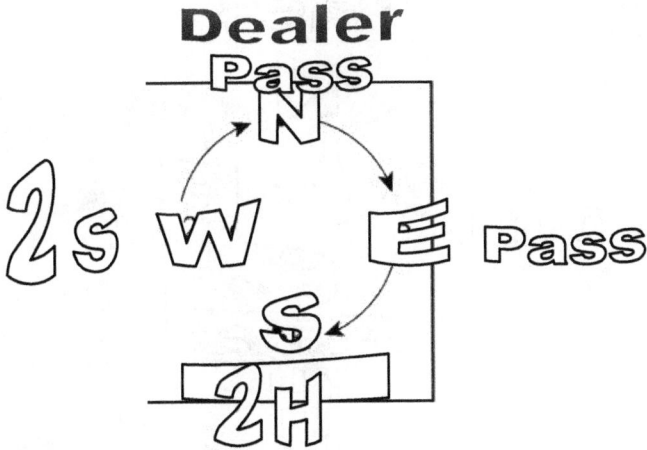

2H + 2S
10 + 10 = 20 Points

In the above example, points are evenly distributed. It will take round two to determine the estimated count. This game will probably produce a part score.

South

♠73
♥KQT754
♣Q
♦JT63

Total Points = 10

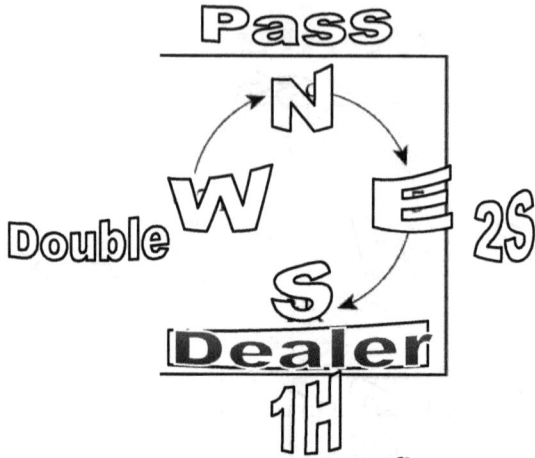

1H + Double + 2S

13+13+10=36

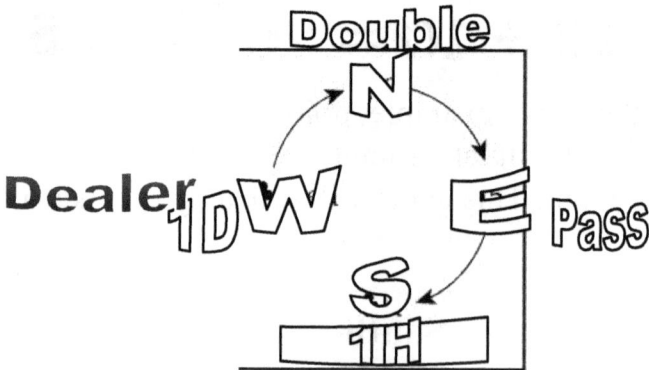

1D + Double + 1H

13+13+6=32

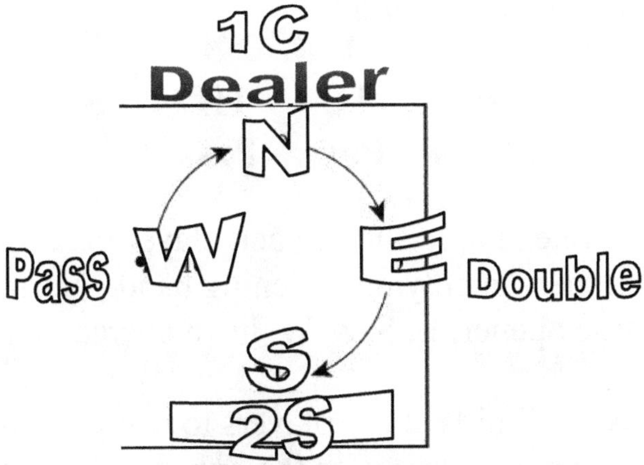

1C

Dealer

N

Pass • W E Double

S

2S

1C + Double + 2S

13 + 13 + 6 = 32

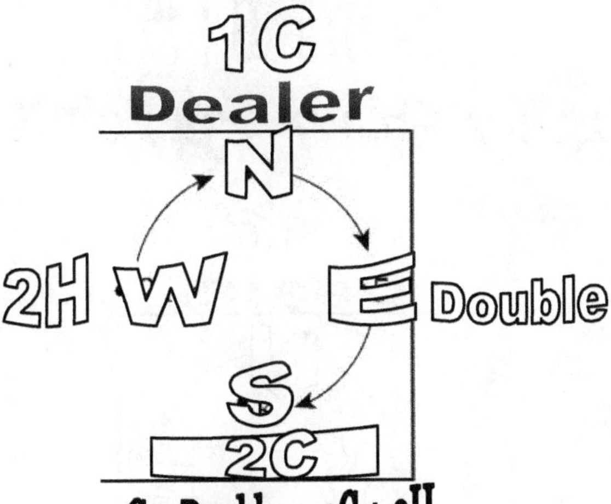

1C

Dealer

N

2H • W E Double

S

2C

1C + Double + 2C + 2H

13 + 13 + 6 + 8 = 40

N	E	S	W
1C	1D	1H	1S
Pass	Pass	Pass	

Above example shows each player making a bid
But, there is only one opening hand. North is the
true opener. E, S, & W have overcall hands.

Overcall bids allow players to compete for the
contract, interfere with the opponent's auction or
help the partnership find the best defense or lead.
Go to page 13, to view Point Chart for Overcall
values.

$$1C + 1D + 1H + 1S$$

$$13 + 7 + 7 + 7 = 34 \text{ Points}$$

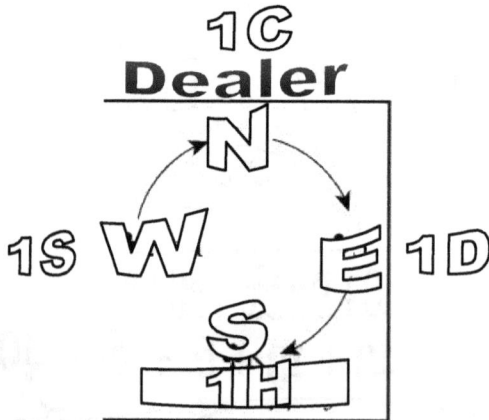

1C
Dealer

1S W E 1D

N

S

1H

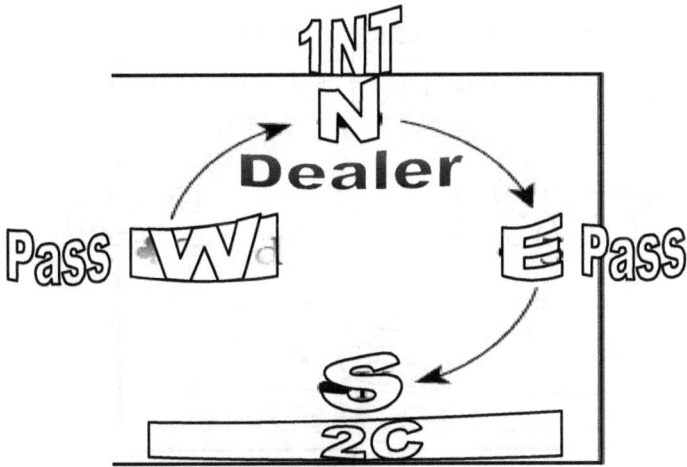

1NT + 2C
15 + 8 = 23 pts

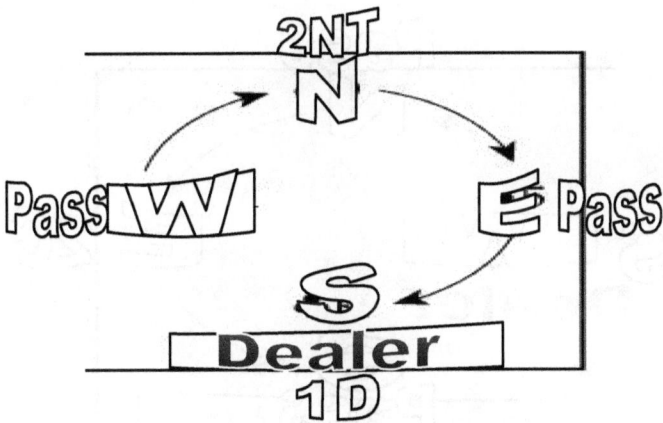

1D + 2NT

13 + 15 = 28 pts

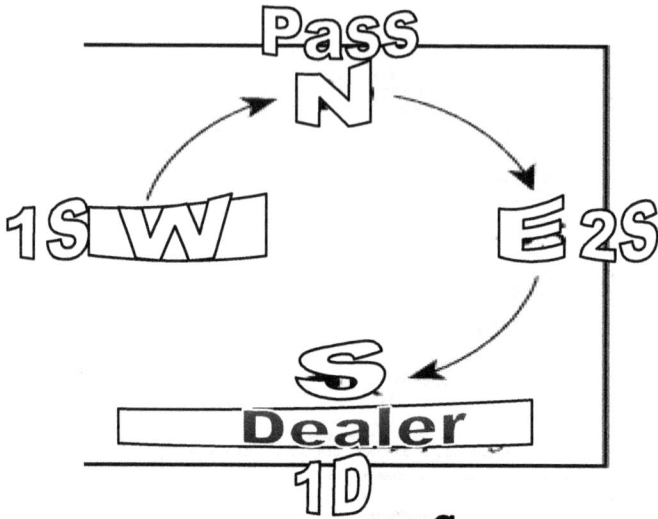

1D + 1S + 2S
13 + 7 + 6 = 26 pts

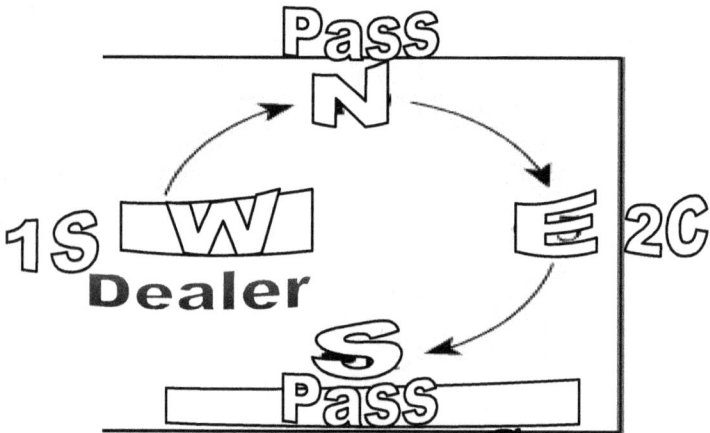

1S + 2C
13 + 9 = 22 pts

Auction Quizzes on Page 61

Dummy Point Count

When Dummy goes down, add your point count to
the Dummy hand.   It displays an extra hand with a
double feature. For example, a player can count
winners & losers while looking at two hands. The
combined hands will come closer to the overall
total of 40 points.

	Spades	Hearts	Diamonds	Clubs
Dummy	KQJ8	JT53	A95	QJ
Your Hand	AT73	A63	532	K86

The combined hands will produce 24 HCP's. This
means that 15 HCP's are with the bad guys. Notice
1 point is wasted in Dummy's hand due to a Club
doubleton. Next, look at the combined hands and
count your sure winners. Four Spades, Two Hearts,
One Diamond, and Two Clubs can be taken without
much trouble. There are 4 losers.

	Spades	Hearts	Diamonds	Clubs
Dummy	JT76	AJ642	7	KJ4
Your Hand	A432	AT7	KQJ	A82

The combined hands have 26 HCP's. Opponents
are left with 13 HCP's. (10 winners & 3 losers)

Solve the following examples

	Spades	Hearts	Diamonds	Clubs
A. Dummy	JT	KQ3	T98654	K98
Your Hand	KQ975	9852	A8	J4

	Spades	Hearts	Diamonds	Clubs
B. Dummy	A4	K654	KJ42	KQ3
Your Hand	KT875	AT3	9	A876

	Spades	Hearts	Diamonds	Clubs
C. Dummy	QT64	T8652	A2	T2
Your Hand	A97532	74	K	AK54

	Spades	Hearts	Diamonds	Clubs
D. Dummy	KJ52	KJ	Q75	AT93
Your Hand	QJ6	86	AKJ63	Q64

Answers on Page 77

Practice Exercises
Identify HCP and Distribution
for Opening Suit Bids
Ace = 4 King = 3 Queen = 2 Jack = 1
Doubleton = 1 Singleton = 2 Void = 3
Add up the following equations by combining the
Honor Cards Symbols (AKQJT) into numbers to obtain
the total point count. Pay no attention to HCP
protection and/or Distributional count.

Solutions on Page 52

1. K+J+Q+A+K =
2. Q+Q+A+A+J =
3. K+K+Q+Q+A=
4. J+K+Q+A+A+K=
5. Q+A+Q+A+A+J=
6. K+Q+J+A+K+K+Q =
7. T+Q+A+A+Q+K+J =
8. A+K+Q+A+J+J+Q =
9. Q+A+Q+A+J+K+Q+T =
10. A+A+Q+A+Q+K+Q+T =
11. A+K+Q+J =
12. K+A+Q+J+Q+A =
13. A+A+Q+K+K+J=
14. Q+J+A+K+J=
15. J+A+J+A+A =
16. A+Q+A+K+T+K+J =
17. J+Q+T+A+Q+K+A =
18. Q+Q+T+A+Q+K+A =
19. A+Q+T+J+Q+K+J+A =
20. A+J+A+T+K+Q+T =

This training exercise is like going to the eye doctor.
Is it blurry or clear? With practice ... it will become perfectly clear.

Practice Exercises
Identify HCP
Opener for **No Trump Bids**
Examine and agree or disagree. Mark your correction
Quizzes on page 57

♠KQ4
♥A6
♣J962
♦KQT5
Total Pts _15

♠KQJ83
♥A9
♣KQ2
♦KQ8
Total Pts 20_

♠AKQ
♥AT
♣AQ3
♦KQJ65
Total Pts _24

♠A983
♥AJ
♣K962
♦KQ8
Total Pts _16

♠AQJ74
♥KQ8
♣KQ
♦AT7
Total Pts _18

♠AQ983
♥AK
♣A962
♦K8
Total Pts _20

Practice Exercises
Identify HCP and Distribution
for Opening **Suit Bids**
Examine and agree or disagree. Mark your correction

♠A5432
♥J93
♣2
♦JT6
Total Pts_6

♠T
♥AJ94
♣AKQT87
♦76
Total Pts _14

♠JT542
♥K873
♣2
♦A82
Total Pts _10

♠875
♥T987
♣T4
♦9764
Total Pts _0

♠T9
♥AJ972
♣AQ87
♦A5
Total Pts _15

♠Q8
♥96
♣53
♦AQ97642
Total Pts _8

Practice Exercises
Identify HCP and Distribution
for Opening **Suit Bids**
Examine and agree or disagree. Mark your correction

♠A
♥QT972
♣JT7
♦AQJ7
Total Pts _14

♠K854
♥QT865
♣QT94
♦VOID
Total Pts _12

♠K85
♥Q92
♣JT863
♦84
Total Pts _ 7

♠AJ32
♥AJ
♣85
♦KQJ75
Total Pt _16

♠AQ4
♥AJ763
♣87
♦875
Total Pts _12

♠64
♥AKT932
♣A96
♦98
Total Pts _ 14

Practice Exercises
Identify HCP
for Opening **No Trump Bids**
Examine and agree or disagree. Mark your correction

♠52
♥KJT974
♣AQ53
♦K
Total Pts _10

♠KQ
♥A96
♣KT732
♦KQ8
Total Pts_15

♠AJT65
♥T8
♣97
♦K653
Total Pts _8

♠AJ5
♥J865
♣Q432
♦K4
Total Pts _11

♠A54
♥A
♣Q32
♦KQJT87
Total Pts _16

♠A983
♥AJ
♣J962
♦8
Total Pts _9

Practice Exercises
Identify HCP and Distribution
for Opening No Trump Bids
Examine and agree or disagree. Mark your correction

♠QJ84
♥J
♣JT6
♦A9532
Total Pts _7

♠KT942
♥62
♣AT765
♦3
Total Pts_7

♠AKJ
♥AQJ
♣VOID
♦KQJ6543
Total Pts _19

♠T983
♥94
♣962
♦T974
Total Pts _0

♠A98
♥AJ87
♣K52
♦Q75
Total Pts _13

♠T9
♥974
♣KT72
♦AJ82
Total Pts _3

Practice Exercises
Identify HCP
for Opening No Trump Bids
Examine and agree or disagree. Mark your correction

♠KJ4
♥K6
♣QJ62
♦AQT5
Total Pts _16

♠QJ863
♥AK
♣KQ4
♦AJ3
Total Pts _20

♠Q85432
♥AQ4
♣Q964
♦VOID
Total Pts _10

♠AQJ63
♥4
♣Q9762
♦KT
Total Pts _11

♠A
♥AK872
♣AK987
♦94
Total Pts _18

♠JT92
♥AQJ7
♣QJ8
♦Q3
Total Pts _10

Practice Exercises
Identify HCP and Distribution
for Opening Suit Bids
Examine and agree or disagree. Mark your correction

♠64
♥AKQJ
♣982
♦K964
HCP 13 **Dist.** 1 Tot 14

♠A982
♥KT653
♣VOID
♦JT73
HCP 8 **Dist.** 3 Tot 11

♠AT987
♥K4
♣A962
♦Q8
HCP 11 **Dist.** 1 Tot 12

♠QJ953
♥84
♣T962
♦K8
HCP 6 **Dist.** 2 Tot 8

♠98543
♥A6
♣A763
♦J8
HCP 8 **Dist.** 1 Tot 9

♠AKQ98
♥A2
♣KJ62
♦85
HCP_17 **Dist**_2 Tot_ 19

The Perfect
No Trump Opener

♣   ♥   ♠   ♦

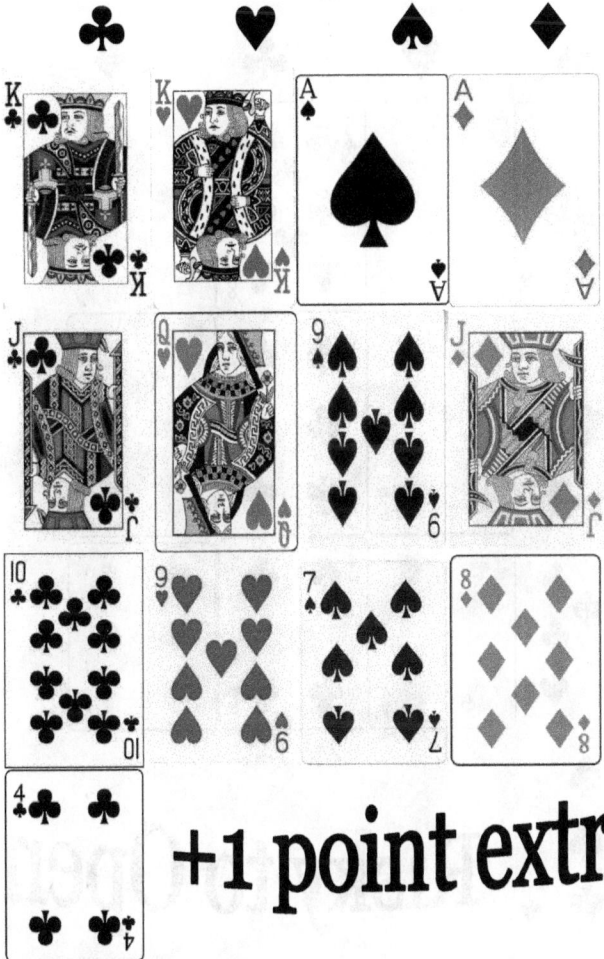

+1 point extra

Notice hand formation distribution
4333

3 Twelve Point Hands in the Orbit of Opening Count!

♠ ♥ ♣ ♦

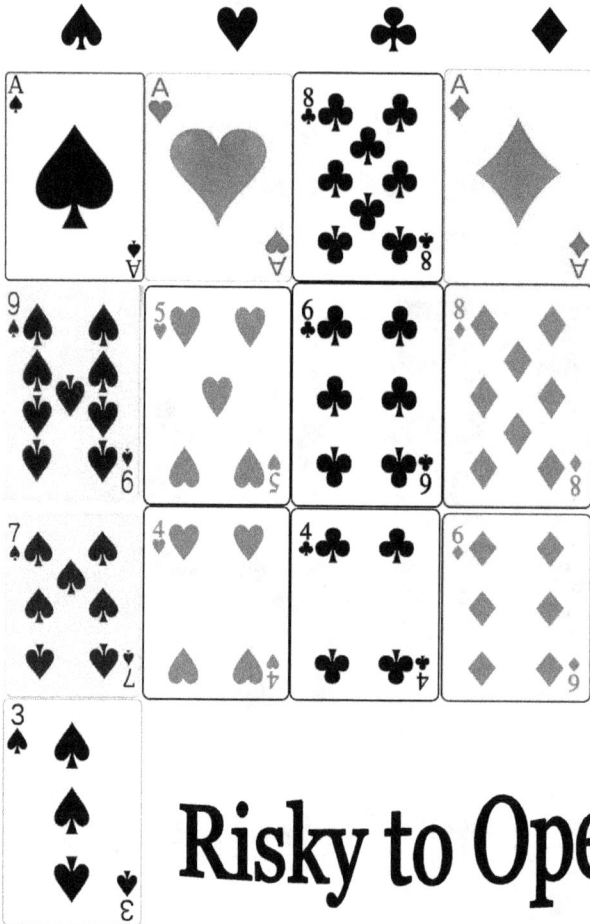

Risky to Open

MAYBE 3ᴿᴰ OR 4ᵀᴴ SEAT OPENER

HAND CAN BE OPENED 3ᴿᴰ OR 4ᵀᴴ SEAT

♠   ♥   ♣   ♦

You Quack me up!

It's risky to open a duck hand full of Queens and Jacks

HAND CAN BE OPENED 3RD OR 4TH SEAT

♠   ♥   ♣   ♦

K♠   K♥   K♣   K♦

7♠   9♥   10♣   8♦

4♠   7♥   8♣   6♦

3♠   **Low Risk to Open**

History

According to Ely Culbertson in The New Gold Book of Bidding and Play – 1936, the origin of **No Trump** can be traced back to the point count system of Milton Work, Bryant McCampbell and Dr. William Pole during the turn of the century, 1890-1905.

Ace = 4   King = 3   Queen = 2   Jack = 1

In 1903, a bridge player named Edmund Roberson branded the point count valuation system as a bridge standard. Only HCP's are counted in NT Bids. Distributional points have no value. For novice players, this adding-machine point count approach is necessary in order to be able to improvise in the later stages of your bridge growth. For now, your partner is counting on you to provide correct information. The rules are simple for opening NT bidding. Your hand must have 15-17 HCPs with balance formation such as (4333, 4432 or 5332) and protection in all suits, unless your partnership is flexible. Also, only HCP have value – not distribution

INSTRUCTIONS

Point Count Table:
ACE—4 points
KING—3 points
QUEEN—2 points
JACK—1 point
Add 1 point for all four Aces
QUICK TRICKS — AK—2 AQ—1½
KQ—1 Kx—½

REQUIREMENTS FOR OPENING BID:

One in a suit:
a. 12 pts. with good rebid and 2 quick tricks.
b. 13 pts. optional.
c. 14 pts.—must open.
Can open in 3rd position with 11 pts. with good suit. No rebid required.

Two in suit:
25 pts. with good 5-card suit.
23 pts. with good 6-card suit.
21 pts. with good 7-card suit.
(1 pt. less, with 2nd good 5-card suit.)

No Trump: (High card values only)
1 NT—16-18 pts.
2 NT—22-24 pts.
3 NT—25-27 pts.
19-21 pts.—Open 1 of suit. Over partner's response, jump in NT.

PREEMPTIVE BIDS:

Do not preempt any hand containing as many as 11 honor pts.
If partner preempts do not bid or raise without value of opening bid.

Distribution Points:
a. For opening bids, count:
3 pts. for void
2 pts. for singleton
1 pt. for doubleton
b. When RAISING Partner's bid, count:
5 pts. for void
3 pts. for singleton
1 pt. for doubleton
NOTE. Add above points under (a) and (b) to value of high cards. Increase, or promote each honor in partner's bid suit by 1 point (unless these honors already total 4 pts.) Deduct 1 point from total distributional values, if hand contains only three trumps, or if hand is distributed 4-3-3-3.

TAKE-OUT DOUBLE:

Doubler's hand should be as good as opening bid, i. e., 13 pts. over a suit bid—16 pts. over 1 N.T.

As Responder to take-out double:
0 to 8 pts.—bid once, except after intervening bid.
9 pts.—may make 1 rebid
11 to 12 pts.—give jump bid

As Partner of opening bidder — after a take-out double, pass with a poor hand, bid immediately with a moderate hand, and redouble with a good hand (10 or more pts.)

TO OVERCALL:

At one level—at least 10 pts.
At two level—at least 12 pts.
To bid 1 NT, must have 16 pts. with NT distribution.

50 Q 41

HEINES - BRUELHEIDE PUBLISHING CO., Inc.
Minneapolis 1, Minnesota
Copyright 1954 by BIDMASTERS

Charles H. Goren Bidding Wheel
Bid Master, CopyRight 1944

One of the best ways to think about making an older system relative is to go back and look at what made it successful to begin with … Just think of Charles H. Goren, who developed the Goren Count Point System, in 1944. This collection of bridge rules has stood the test of time. Bridge players relied on the point count system to determine if a player should bid or pass. By following Goren tips from long ago, a novice player should be able to compile plenty of Master Points.

13-14 point is a mandatory bid

Required points for game=26 HCP

Contact bid 4 ♠ or 4 ♥ = 26 HCP + distribution

Contract bid 5 ♣ or 5 ♦ = 29 HCP + distribution

6 NT = 33 - 34 HCP

6 of any Suit Bid = 33-34 points

7 of any Suit Bid =37 points

Suit Ranking

Spade	**Heart**	**Diamond**	**Club**
highest	2nd highest	3rd highest	lowest
♠ →	♥ →	♦ →	♣

Word Cloud

Opener 13
Double 13
My Hand 9
35 Points

The Fit

Does counting points play a role in finding an 8+ card major suit fit? If so, does it play a role in holding your partner accountable for responding to your opening bid.

The answer to these questions are based on the opener having enough points (13+ points), and partner having 6+ points to respond. The partnership should always try to find the longest suit between the two hands. But, having the correct point count is required. The combined hands of … at least 8 cards in a major suit, is called a **Fit.**

Example

South	North
South	**North**

♠A 5 3 2   ♠ 8 7 5 4
♥A J 8   ♥ K Q 3
♦7 6   ♦ A T 6
♣K Q T 3   ♣ A J 4

These two hands have a fit in Spades. Note that a fit is determined by the number of cards held. The fit does not require high cards in the Fit suit. Once again, opener must have 13+points and responder must have 6+ points.

South	North
♠ 8 5	♠ Q J T 8
♥ K J T 8 5	♥ Q 9 7
♦ J 9 5 4	♦ 7 5 3
♣ K J	♣ A Q T

Can you find the fit for this partnership? **Hearts**

Sometimes, there is no fit within the partnership.
Even though 25-28 points may exist between
North & South, their hands may not fit together.

South	North
♠ A 5 3	♠ Q J 4 2
♥ K J 7 6	♥ Q
♦ K T 5 4	♦ Q J 8 3
♣ 6 2	♣ K J T 7

Partnership Total point = 25
South 13   North 12

This hand is possible for game. But, there is not a suit
fit because the hand lacks of 8+ cards major suit.
3 NT game will require 9 tricks. So far, only 7 exist.

NORTH (DEALER)
♠A876
♥A764
♦T94
♣K7

WEST
♠32
♥3
♦Q872
♣QJT852

EAST
♠ JT
♥ KJ92
♦ AKJ
♣ 9643

SOUTH
♠KQ954
♥QT85
♦653
♣A

Bidding E/W Vulnerable

NORTH	EAST	SOUTH	WEST
PASS	PASS	1S	PASS
2S	PASS	PASS	PASS

THIRD PLAYER OPENS LIGHT. NORTH SHOWS A SPADE FIT. BUT, GAME IS FOOLS GOAL BECAUSE N/S COMBINED ONLY HAVE 22/23 POINTS.

King Mojito

1 1/2 oz White Rum
6 Mint Leaves
Soda Water
1 oz Lime Juice
2 Tsp Sugar

Muddle Mint Leaves with sugar and lime juice.
Add rum and top with soda water.
Mint leave garnish & serve with a straw.

Cosmopolitan Queen

2 ounces vodka
1 ounce triple sec
1 ounce cranberry juice
1/2 ounce lime juice
Lime Wedge

Fill cocktail shaker 1/2 full with ice
add vodka, triple sec & juices, shake
until blended, strain into chilled martini glass
Garnish with lime wedge

Jack Hammer

Jack Daniels
&
Amaretto

This drink is a great
choice to unwind after
a rough bridge game session.

Dealer
1 Club 13

Overcall
1 Heart 7

My Hand 13

33 Points

Word Cloud

Telephone Number

Simple Question: If Declarer knows where the majority of the points are located, then why is it necessary to keep counting?

A bridge player will continue to count until the game is over. Even when Dummy goes down, Declarer will make a plan by developing a telephone number from the opponent's combined hands. By adding 2 hands together, Declarer will derive at a four number code called the Telephone Number.

Ask yourself, what is the distribution **double** count of the opponent's hand? Distribution in this sense means, the shape of the hand, i.e. number of Spades, Hearts, Diamonds, and Clubs?

	♠	♥	♣	♦
Dummy	KJ8	AQ82	987	T74
Declarer	T75	KJT9	KQT96	A

1.

Telephone Number is 7559. It represents 7 Spades, 5 Hearts, 5 Clubs, 9 Diamonds in the Opponent's Hand. This number is helpful in finding winners and losers in certain suits.

		♠	♥	♣	♦
2.	Dummy	QJT45	AJT	K864	A
	South	AK97	42	JT72	KQJ

Telephone Number

		♠	♥	♣	♦
3.	Dummy	QJ4	AJT7	QT8	KJ9
	South	T9	KQ642	A94	AQT

Telephone Number is

		♠	♥	♣	♦
4.	Dummy	AQJ3	82	942	7643
	Declarer	K	QJT963	A85	JT8

Telephone Number is

		♠	♥	♣	♦
5.	Dummy	K85	J932	JT3	JT7
	South	J4	75	A9652	A942

Telephone Number is

	♠	♥	♣	♦
6. Dummy	AQJT	VOID	A865	JT932
Declarer	5432	KT62	K2	A65

Telephone Number is

	♠	♥	♣	♦
7. Dummy	AK	AQT9	KQT6	AT3
Declarer	QJT962	984	73	54

Telephone Number is

	♠	♥	♣	♦
8. Dummy	K85	J932	JT3	JT7
Declarer	J4	75	A9652	A942

Telephone Number is

	♠	♥	♣	♦
9. Dummy	KJ95	AK842	KQ	Q4
Declarer	AQT876	9873	J5	A6

Telephone Number is

		♠	♥	♣	♦
10.	Dummy	876	AQJ5	8765	43
	Declarer	AKJT9	62	K43	KJ6

Telephone Number is

		♠	♥	♣	♦
11.	Dummy	JT	KQ3	T98654	K98
	Declarer	KQ975	9852	A8	J4

Telephone Number is

		♠	♥	♣	♦
12.	Dummy	KQJ8	JT53	A95	QJ
	Declarer	AT73	A63	532	K86

Telephone Number is

		♠	♥	♣	♦
13.	Dummy	96	K43	K85	AKJT5
	Declarer	K5	AJ72	AQ32	643

Telephone Number is

		♠	♥	♣	♦
14.	Dummy	JT76	AJ642	7	KJ4
	Declarer	A432	AT7	KQJ	A82

Telephone Number is

		♠	♥	♣	♦
15.	Dummy	A4	K654	KJ42	KQ3
	Declarer	KT875	AT3	9	A876

Telephone Number is

		♠	♥	♣	♦
16.	Dummy	QT64	T8652	A2	T2
	Declarer	A97532	74	K4	AK3

Telephone Number is

		♠	♥	♣	♦
17	Dummy	KJ32	KJ	Q75	AT93
	Declarer	QJ6	86	AKJ63	Q64

Telephone Number is

Telephone Number Answers

1. 7559
2. 4859
3. 8478
4. 8576
5. 8756
6. 5975
7. 5678
8. 8756
9. 3499
10. 5768
11. 6658
12. 5678
13. 9665
14. 5597
15. 6686
16. 3697
17. 6956

The prime directive of the Telephone Number is to identify and track good and bad suits.

1. 13   2. 13   3. 14   4. 18   5. 17

6. 18   7. 16   8. 17   9. 18   10. 21

11. 10   12. 16   13. 17   14. 11   15. 14

16. 17   17. 17   18. 16   19. 17   20. 14

Answers on Page 23

More Count Equations on Page 90

Tom Collins U're a Real ACE

2 oz Gin
1 oz Lemon Juice
3 oz Club Soda
2 Tsp Super-Fine Sugar
Maraschino Cherry
Orange Slice

Fill shaker 1/2 full with ice
Add Gin, Lemon Juice & Sugar.
Shake until blended, strain into
ice-filled Collins glass. Fill glass with
Club Soda. Cherry & Orange Slice garnish

Word Cloud

1 NT 15
2 Clubs 6
My Hand 5
26 Points

Player's Hand
Auction
Dummy's Hand

Word Cloud

COUNTING PAD

Point Count Paths

Player

Auction

Dummy

Keep Your Brain Alive, Play Bridge!

Personal Count QUIZZES
Margin of error + or − 1 point

	♠	♥	♦	♣	TOTAL
1.	QJT98	QJT98	QJ	Q =	__
2.	QJT9	QJT	QJT	QJT =	__
3.	QJ63	QJ5	QJ4	QJ5 =	__
4.	A632	A53	A43	542 =	__
5.	QJ2	QJT94	AQ	QJ3 =	__
6.	AKJ63	873	42	A42 =	__
7.	AT632	964	K4	A73 =	__
8.	T63	AQJ75	A85	93 =	__
9.	Q73	A9753	A54	J3 =	__
10.	AK973	VOID	Q54	QT973 =	__
11.	K96	A963	AJ94	AK =	__
12.	73	T	KQT8	JT8543 =	__

58

	♠	♥	♦	♣	TOTAL
13.	K2	AK875	AQ9	KQT	= __
14.	AKT9	AK	Q52	A873	= __
15.	982	A853	K84	AK9	= __
16.	Q6	QT82	T74	AKJT	= __
17.	93	JT	T9652	A854	= __
18.	52	A2	KQJT742	T5	= __
19.	63	T876	J8	AQ632	= __
20.	A7	52	K9763	AT93	= __
21.	75	K43	AJ853	982	= __
22.	A643	AT	A7	AQ853	= __
23.	QT3	QT7	A4	AJT64	= __
24.	AK973	VOID	Q54	QT652	= __

	♠	♥	♦	♣	TOTAL
25.	J2	A862	AKT	AJ96	= __
26.	AQT5	AQ	K52	Q863	= __
27.	T43	AQJ843	AK8	9	= __
28.	A632	A53	A43	542	= __
29.	K	KT95	32	KQJ742	= __
30.	74	9432	T832	Q72	= __
31.	A2	AJT732	75	A74	= __
32.	8	987532	T943	A6	= __
33.	T732	K2	AKQ	AK64	= __
34.	KQT72	K98	KJ873	VOID	= __
35.	QJ32	J	A3	AKQJ63	= __
36.	AQ8653	KT83	82	4	= __

♠	♥	♦	♣	TOTAL
37. QJ98	QJT8	AQJ	KQ	= __
38. AQJT9	JT	AQJT6	T	= __
39. KJ63	KQJ5	VOID	AQJ5	= __
40. AK32	A53	A43	K5	= __
41. QJ2	QJT94	AQ	QJ3	= __
42. A63	873	7642	A42	= __
43. QT632	96	K4	JT73	= __
44. QJ63	AKJ75	A	T93	= __
45. VOID	AK753	A54	A	= __
46. AK973	KT	Q54	KJ973	= __
47. KT6	T963	9764	82	= __
48. T3	T	AKQT8	KT8543	= __

Answers on Page 69

Auction Flow Chart Quizzes

1.

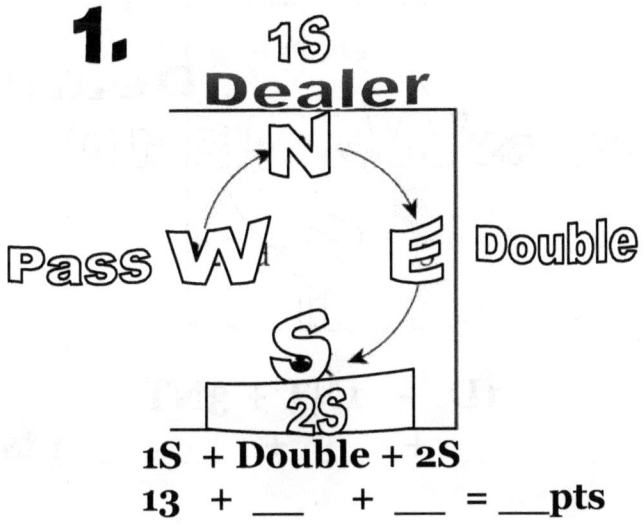

1S + Double + 2S

13 + __ + __ = __pts

2.

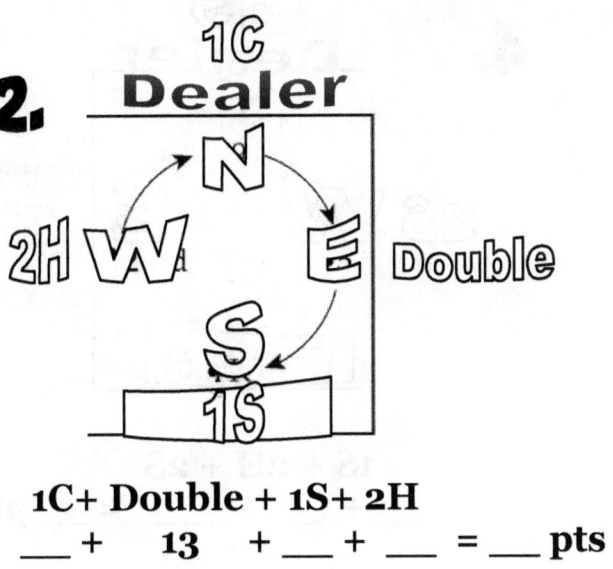

1C+ Double + 1S+ 2H

__ + 13 + __ + __ = __ pts

3.

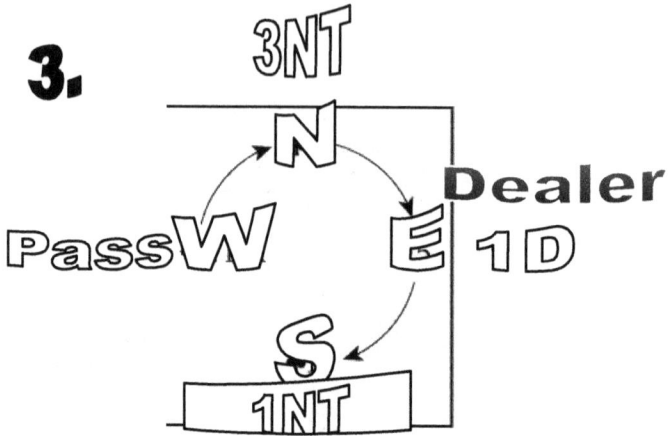

3NT

N

Dealer

Pass W   E 1D

S

1NT

1D + 1NT + 3NT

__ + __ + __ = __ pts

4.

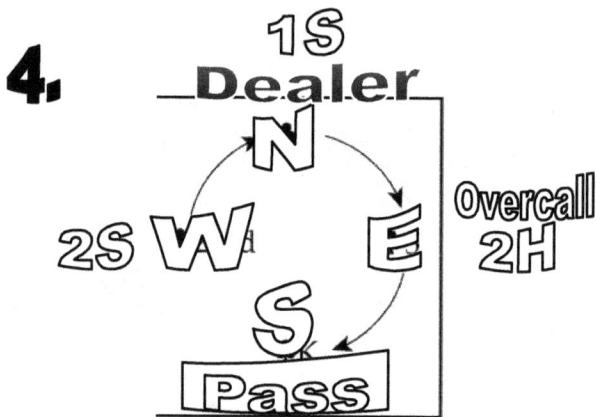

1S

Dealer

N

Overcall
2H

2S W   E

S

Pass

1S + 2H + 2S

__ + __ + ___ = __ pts

5.

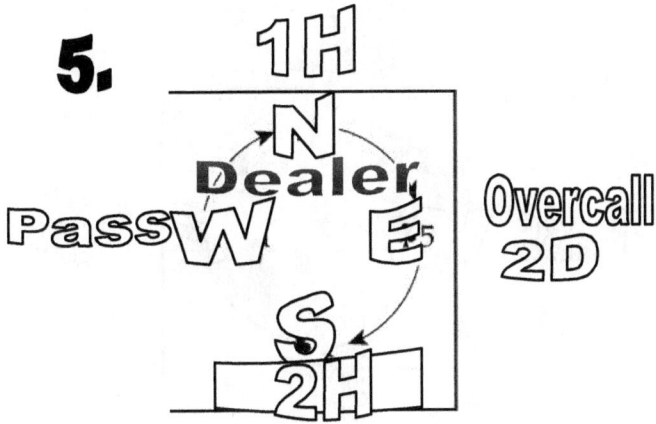

1H + 2D + 2H

___ + ___ + ___ = ___ pts

6.

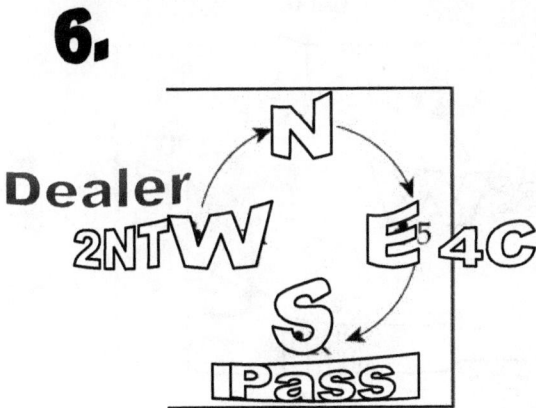

2NT + 4C

___ + ___ = ___ pts

7.

1NT

N

Dealer

Pass W   E Pass

S

2NT

1NT + 2NT

___ + ___ = ___ pts

8.

1NT

N

Dealer

Pass W   E Pass

S

3NT

1NT + 3NT

___ + ___ = ___ pts

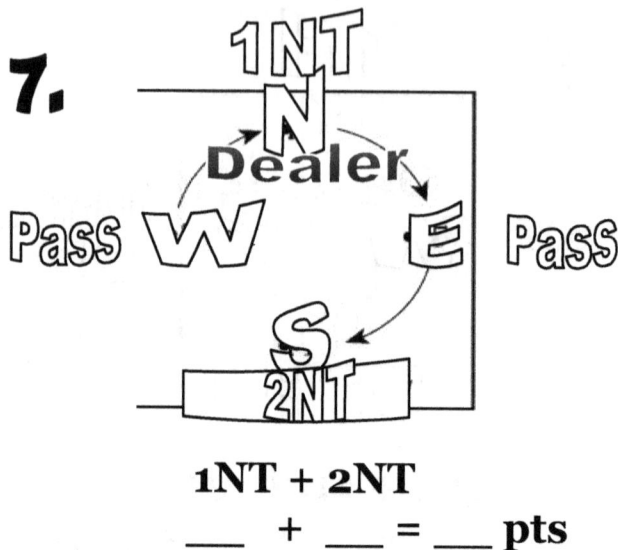

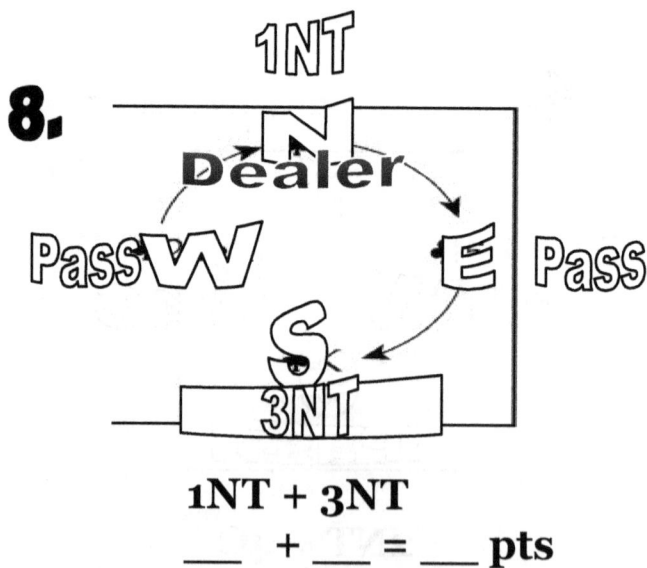

Answers on Page 71

Dummy Count QUIZZES

RHO Doubles during Round One of bidding. Your side won the auction. 3 Heart Contract.

	♠	♥	♣	♦
1. Dummy	KJ8	AQ82	987	T74
Declarer	T75	KJT9	KQT96	A

Total Points

Dummy ___ + Declarer ___ + RHO =

∿∿∿

LHO/Dealer opens 2 Diamonds. South won the auction. 4 Spade contract.

	♠	♥	♣	♦
2. Dummy	QJT45	AJT	K864	A
South	AK97	42	JT72	KQJ

Total Points

Dummy ___ + South ___ + LHO =

∿∿∿

RHO made an Overcall 1 Spade bid. West won the auction. 4 Hearts Contract.

	♠	♥	♣	♦
3. Dummy	QJ4	AJT7	QT8	KJ9
South	T9	KQ642	A94	AQT

Total Points

Dummy ___ + South ___ + RHO =

North opens with 2 Hearts, and won the auction.

	♠	♥	♣	♦
4. Dummy	AQJ3	82	942	7643
Declarer	K	QJT963	A85	JT8

Total Points

Dummy ___ + Declarer ___ + RHO =

^^^

South , Dealer - West opens 1 Spade. East respond 2 Spades.   This leads to a 4 Spade Contract.

	♠	♥	♣	♦
5. Dummy	K85	J932	JT3	JT7
South	J4	75	A9652	A942

Declarer's hand is up.   Total Points

Dummy ___ + South ___ + Declarer ___ =

^^^

RHO bids 1 Heart .Auction won by South .   3NT

	♠	♥	♣	♦
6. Dummy	AQJT	VOID	A865	JT932
South	5432	KT62	K2	A65

Total Points

Dummy ___ + South ___ + RHO =

LHO opens 1NT.   Your side N/S won the auction.

	♠	♥	♣	♦
7. Dummy	AK	AQT9	KQT6	AT3
Declarer	QJT0962	84	73	54

Total Points

Dummy ___ + Declarer ___ + LHO __ =

∧∧

South , Dealer - West opens 1 Spade. East respond
2 Spades. This leads to a 4 Spade Contract.

	♠	♥	♣	♦
8. Dummy	K85	J932	JT3	JT7
South	J4	75	A9652	A942

Declarer's hand is up.   Total Points

Dummy ___+ South ___+ Declarer ___ =

∧∧

RHO made an Overcall 1 Spade bid. West won the
auction. 4 Hearts Contract.

	♠	♥	♣	♦
9. Dummy	KJ95	AK842	KQ	Q4
South	AQJT86	9873	J5	A6

Total Points

Dummy ___ + South ___ + RHO =

North opens 1NT. Contract is 6NT.

	♠	♥	♣	♦

10. Dummy   KJ9   AQ3   Q94   KQJ2

Total Points

Dummy ___ + Declarer ___ =

∧∧∧∧∧∧∧∧∧∧∧∧∧∧∧∧∧∧∧∧∧∧∧∧∧∧∧∧∧∧∧∧∧∧∧∧∧∧

North opens 1 Diamond. Contract is 6 Diamonds.

	♠	♥	♣	♦

11. Dummy   A   T82   KQJT863 AQ5

Total Points

Dummy ___ + Declarer ___ =

∧∧∧∧∧∧∧∧∧∧∧∧∧∧∧∧∧∧∧∧∧∧∧∧∧∧∧∧∧∧∧∧∧∧∧∧∧∧

North opens 1 Heart.   Contract is 6 Hearts.

	♠	♥	♣	♦

12. Dummy   AKQ   A72   QJT7   KQJ

Total Points

Dummy ___ + Declarer ___ =

North opens 1 Spade. Contract is 4 Spades.

	♠	♥	♣	♦

13. Dummy   AQJT9   JT   AQJT6   T

Dummy ___ + Declarer ___

Answers on Page 72

Hand Point Count Quizzes Answers

1. 9 2. 12 3. 12 4. 12 5. 14

6. 12 7. 11 8. 11 9. 11 10. 14

11. 20 12. 9 13. 21 14. 20 15. 14

16. 11 17. 6 18. 12 19. 8 20. 12

21. 9 22. 18 23. 14 24. 14 25. 17

26. 18 27. 16 28. 12 29. 12 30. 3

31. 14 32. 6 33. 17 34. 15 35. 19

36. 12 37. 15 38. 15 39. 19 40. 18

41. 15 42. 8 43. 7 44. 17 45. 20

46. 16 47. 0 48. 19

Remember,
the 1st round of bidding will provide a
large portion of the points than any
auction round. Sometimes, a 2nd or 3rd
round is required to confirm point total.

Like a Venn Diagram which shows the
relationship between different groups,
the Player's hand, the Auction, and the
Dummy have an overlapping counting
relationship. This relationship is called
a Harmonic Conversion. It's when your
hand makes sense.

HC = Harmonic Conversion

Auction Flow Chart Answers

1. 1S+ Double + 2S
    13 + 13 + 6 = 32 pts

2. 1C+ Double + 1S+ 2H
    13 + 13 + 6 + 6 = 38 pts

3. 1D + 1NT + 3NT
    13 + 10 + 13 = 36 pts

4. 1S + 2H + 2S
    13 + 7 + 13 = 33 pts

5. 1H + 2D + 2H
    13 + 7 + 6 = 26 pts

6. 2NT + 4C
    20 + 13 = 33 pts

7. 1NT + 2NT
    15 + 8 = 23 pts

8. 1NT + 3NT
    15 + 13 = 28 pts

Dummy Count QUIZZES Answers

1. Dummy 10 + Declarer 14 + RHO 13 =37
2. Dummy 16 + Declarer 13 + LHO 5 = 34
3. Dummy 12 + Declarer 15 + RHO 5 =29
4. Dummy 8 + Declarer 8 = 16
5. Dummy 4 + Declarer 13 + South 8 = 25
6. Dummy 15 + South 10 + RHO 13 = 38
7. Dummy 22 + Declarer 3 + LHO 15 =40
8. Dummy 4 + South 8 + Declarer 13 =25
9. Dummy 14 + South 11 + RHO 7 = 32
10. Dummy 18 + Declarer 13 = 33
11. Dummy 18 + Declarer 13 = 31
12. Dummy 21 + Declarer 13 = 34
13. Dummy 17 + Declarer 13 = 30

16 Face Cards Equals 40 Points

Bonus Hand

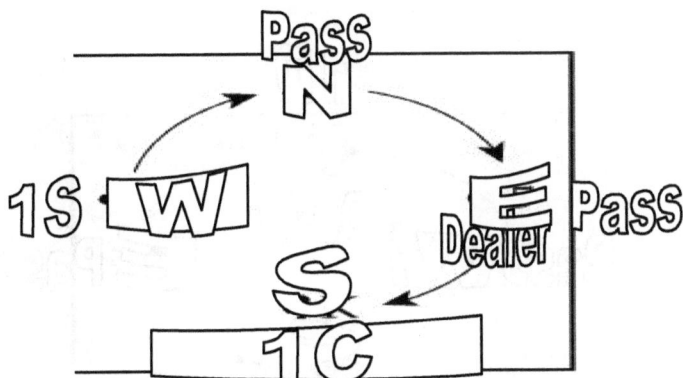

	♠	♥	♣	♦	Total pts

North

T853	AQ3	2	J9864	= 9

South

J7	J42	KJ8753	AQ	= 11

West

K9642	T65	AQ6	T2	= 9

East

AQ	K987	T94	K753	= 11

1C + 1S
13 + 7 = 20 pts

**Even Point Count between partnerships.
This round should be Passed Out!**

Losing Trick Count

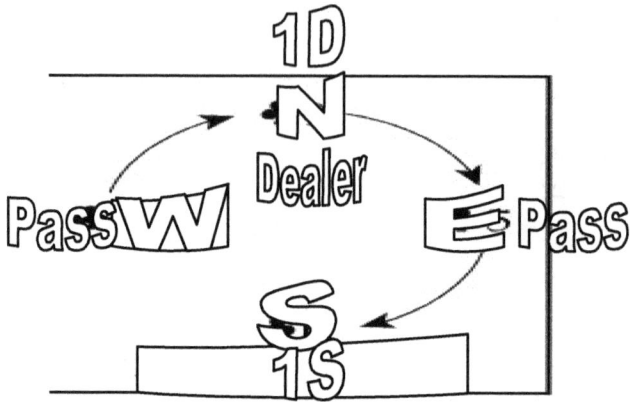

South has 7 HCP's, about 11 or so counting distribution. North has about 19-20. Here are the 2 hands.

North

♠ AQ74   ♥ J8   ♣ K5   ♦ AK943 = 19

South

♠ K86542   ♥ 4   ♣ A943   ♦ 72 = 11

At round 2 of the auction, North jumps to 4 Spades.

It is at this point, the decision to go for Slam using LTC will occur. The combined hands total 30 points.   According to Ron Klinger, the search for Slam is risky when point count is below average. The normal range for Slam is between 33-37 points. The only way to find an excuse for bidding small slam is to use LTC.

LTC is when your partnership's trump suit has been established. And, there is 8 or more trump between the partnership. The formula is to count your losers, add partner's losers, deduct from 24, and the difference is the trick count your side could make.   It works well when each player has some ruffing (trumping) potential.

Unpacking the case above, Spades are trump. Then next step is to count losers. North counts 4 losers, and concludes at least 8 losers in South's hand. The total is substracted from 24. The chart for calculating losers, and how the factor of 24 works in the equation is found in Ron Klinger's Book.

4 North losers + 8 South losers = 12

$$24 - 12 = 12 \text{ Tricks}$$

The result is the number of tricks
they can expect to make.

The point of this example is to show that the
first round of bidding establishes the go-ahead.
It is the same for all first round auctions. This
particular convention (LTC) relies on the shape
and fit of the combined hands rather than
HCP's. It is risky but the benefits could be
worth it.

N	E	S	W
1D	Pass	1S	Pass
4S	Pass	4NT	Pass
5H	Pass	6S	

May all your Slams Be Grand

Dummy Count Solution

Page 22 Examples

A. 4♠ 3♥ 1♦ 1♣ = 9 winners & 4 losers

Combined hands 17 HCP's + 3 Dist. = 20 pts

B. 3♠ 2♥ 1♦ 3♣ = 9 winners & 4 losers

Combined hands 27 HCP's + 3 Dist. = 30 pts

C. 5♠ 0♥ 2♦ 2♣ = 9 winners & 4 losers

Combined hands 17 HCP's + 5 Dist. = 22pts

D. 3♠ 1♥ 4♦ 2♣ = 10 winners & 3 losers

Combined hands 26 HCP's + 1 Dist. = 27 pts

AfterWords

**Learn the counting basics
by using this book as
a reference. Then, add
colorful nuances such as
bidding conventions, i.e., Stayman,
Jacoby Transfer, Blackwood, Splinter,
Two Over One , LTC, etc …**

**Remember, what we don't know about
counting is far, far greater than what we
do know.**

**The 1st source of point counting comes
from a player's hand. And, the input from
all four players come from the auction
round table. Finally, the waterfall of
counting information is when the Dummy
goes down. It shows strengths,
weaknesses, winners and losers. By
absorbing these counting skills, and
sharing the information with your
partner, will put your bridge game in
turn around.**

Word Cloud

1 Club 13
1 Diamond 7
1 Heart 7
1 Spade 7
34 Points

Smile, your partner will play better

The Rule of 15

This rule allows a player to open the bidding after 3 passes if HCP's plus the number of Spades total 15 or more.

♠ A9852 ♥ 95 ♦ AQ97 ♣J4

11 HCP's **+** 5
Spades does satisfy the rule of 15

By the way, a player is not required to open using either Rule 15 or 20.

The Rule of 20

♠ QT9 ♥ VOID ♦ KT985 ♣AJ765 = 10points

This hand contains 10 HCP's and 10 cards in the two longest suits. This adds up to the 20 Rule. Open 1 Club, with any reasonable auction luck, you will end up in 5 Clubs.

♠KT98 ♥ J53 ♦AK873 ♣T = 11 HCPs

4 ♠'s + 5 ♦'s

Hand satisfies the Rule of 20

♠75 ♥ KQT97 ♦ KQ542 ♣T = 10 HCPs

5 ♥'s + 5 ♦'s

Hand satisfies the Rule of 20

♠QT8 ♥ AJ5 ♦ 87 ♣KJ742 = 11 HCPs

5 ♣'s + 3 ♥'s

Hand does not satisfy the Rule of 20

Let's Do The Math

Bridge is a partnership game where players rely upon timely communications. According to Eddie Kantar in the "Gamesman Bridge", players with the best intentions often forget the language of the game. Bridge talk is very limited.

You have 8 nouns,

No Trump, Spade, Heart, Diamond, Club, Double, Redouble, and Pass and 7 adjectives, One, Two, Three, Four, Five, Six, and Seven which combine to form a total of only 38 phrases to describe the 635,013,559,600 possible hands in bridge. By bidding your hand correctly is only half of the equation. Partnership understanding is the other half.

Point Counter-Point

Let's circle back to distributional points, Pg 11. Since 40 is the threshold for total points per deal, then it can be concluded that distributional points are a subset of HCP's. Consequently, distributional points may either peel off value from HCP's or surrender value to HCP's. In other words, points are transferred from one player's hand to another player's hand depending on the final contract. Take the example below, Player A long Spade suit has a better chance to scoop up the 2 points from Player's B hand because the Queen of Spades in not protected. In turn, the point value lost goes to Player A simply by the lopsided number of Spades.

Player A - Spade Suit: AKJT642 **Long Suit**
Only 6 Spades are left among the other 3 players.

Player B - Spades Suit: Q9 **Short Suit**
Since the Queen is not protected, the 2 points is shifted to the player with the long suit.

Here are more examples of Point vs Counter Point.

Player A - Club Suit: AQJT853 **Long Suit**
Ace of Clubs cancels King in Player's B hand.

Player B - Spades Suit: K **Short Suit**
Since the King is not protected, the 3 points is
shifted to Player A hand.

Player A - Hearts Suit: AKQ
The first 3 tricks of this suit are blocked.

Player B - Spades Suit: J
Since the Jack is not protected, the 1 points is
shifted to Player A

Although novice players may not understand every
bridge detail, they should be able to scrutinize each
hand by breaking down point total, suit count, and
auction activity. After establishing a counting
routine, it should become commonplace for a
player's bridge game.

Distributional points = A

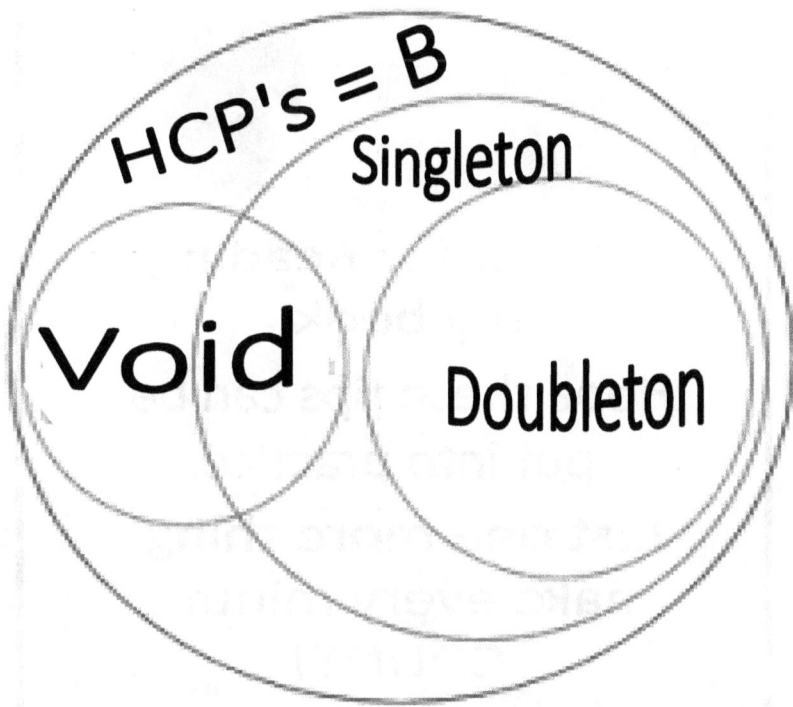

HCP's = B

Singleton

Void

Doubleton

A is a subset of B

Harmonic Conversion

Thanks for Reading my book.

Hope these tips can be put into practice.

Just one more thing, make every minute COUNT!

Butch

Notes

Buzz Words

Personal Count	Auction
Dummy	Forty
Fit	Pad
Point Count	Telephone Number
Distribution	Losing Trick Count
1st Bid Round	Rule of 15 & 20
Singleton	Doubleton
Thirteen	Void

Notes

Extra Count Equations

1. A+J+A+T+K+Q+T=

2. J+A+J+A+A=

3. K+K+Q+Q+A=

4. A+K+Q+A+J+J+Q =

5. Q+A+Q+A+A+J=

6. K+Q+J+A+K+K+Q =

7. T+Q+A+A+Q+K+J =

8. A+A+Q+K+K+J=

9. Q+A+Q+A+J+K+Q+T =

10. A+A+Q+A+Q+K+Q+T =

11. A+J+A+Q+K+Q+T =

12. Q+A+Q+A+Q+K+Q+J =

13. A+A+Q+K+Q+J=

14. A+T+Q+K+K+J=

15. T+A+Q+K+K+J=

16. A+K+Q+J+T=

17. K+A+Q+J+Q+A=

18. Q+Q+A+T+J=

19. Q+J+A+T+K+J=

20. J+K+Q+T+A+K=

21. A+Q+A+K+T+K+J =

22. J+Q+T+A+Q+K+A =

23. Q+Q+T+A+Q+K+A =

24. A+Q+T+J+Q+T+J+A =

25. K+J+Q+A+K+T=

26. A+A+Q+A+Q+K+Q+T =

27. A+Q+A+K+T+K+J =

28. A+A+Q+K+K+J=

29. Q+A+Q+Q+K+J+A=

30. A+J+Q+T+K+J+Q+A=

1.	**14**	16.	**10**
2.	**14**	17.	**16**
3.	**14**	18.	**9**
4.	**17**	19.	**11**
5.	**17**	20.	**17**
6.	**14**	21.	**17**
7.	**16**	22.	**16**
8.	**17**	23.	**17**
9.	**20**	24.	**14**
10.	**21**	25.	**13**
11.	**17**	26.	**21**
12.	**20**	27.	**17**
13.	**18**	28.	**17**
14.	**13**	29.	**18**
15.	**13**	30.	**17**